THE PHILIPPINES

From a portrait owned by the Yale Club, New York

WILLIAM H. TAFT
CIVIL GOVERNOR OF THE PHILIPPINES

THE PHILIPPINES

THE FIRST CIVIL GOVERNOR
BY THEODORE ROOSEVELT

CIVIL GOVERNMENT IN THE PHILIPPINES
BY WILLIAM H. TAFT
CIVIL GOVERNOR OF THE PHILIPPINES

NEW YORK
THE OUTLOOK COMPANY
1902

PUBLISHERS' NOTE

GOVERNOR TAFT'S survey of what
has been already accomplished in the
Philippines in establishing civil government is the best possible indication of
what may be done in the future in ex-
tending and completing the work. The
importance of a full knowledge of actual conditions is apparent; and no-
where have the facts been stated so
fully and so authoritatively as they are
here by Governor Taft. When this
review of the situation was published
in The Outlook (May 31, 1902) the

[5]

editors of that journal pointed out that
it was because they regarded General
Taft as the first expert in the service
of the country in the affairs of the
Philippines that they had asked him to
prepare for their readers a full survey
of what had been accomplished, and an
outline of the policy which he wishes
to have pursued in dealing with the
islands. It is for the same reason
that it has seemed well worth while
to give permanent form to this history
of the laying of the foundations of
American civilization in the Philippines.

The qualities of Judge Taft's character and the nature of his experience
which made him the choice of President
McKinley are admirably brought out in

[6]

President Roosevelt's personal sketch
of "The First Civil Governor." This
characteristically direct and vigorous
appreciation was written a very few
weeks before the assassination of President McKinley, and was first published
in The Outlook of September 21, 1901.

THE FIRST CIVIL GOVERNOR:
WILLIAM H. TAFT

BY THEODORE ROOSEVELT
President of the United States

THE FIRST CIVIL GOVERNOR

A YEAR[1] ago a man of wide acquaintance both with American
public life and American public
men remarked that the first Governor of the Philippines ought to
combine the qualities which would
make a first-class President of the
United States with the qualities
which would make a first-class
Chief Justice of the United States,
and that the only man he knew
who possessed all these qualities

[1] This article was written for The Outlook in
the summer of 1901 by President Roosevelt, then
Vice-President.

[11]

was Judge William H. Taft, of Ohio. The statement was entirely correct. Few more difficult tasks have devolved upon any man of our nationality during our century and a quarter of public life than the handling of the Philippine Islands just at this time; and it may be doubted whether among men now living another could be found as well fitted as Judge Taft to do this incredibly difficult work. Judge Taft belongs to a family which has always done valuable public service. He graduated from Yale in 1878; and a few years later, when Yale gave him the honorary degree of LL.D., he was the youngest of her graduates upon whom she had ever conferred this honor. On graduation he took up the study of the law, and also entered actively into public life. In both careers he rose steadily and rapidly. Under President Harrison he was made Solicitor-General of the United States, and he left this place to become a Judge of the United States District Court.

But his weight in public life was something entirely apart from the office he at any time happened to hold. I dislike speaking in hyperbole; but I think that almost all men who have been brought in close contact, personally and officially, with Judge Taft are agreed that he combines as very, very few men ever can combine, a standard of absolutely unflinching rectitude on every point of public duty, and a literally dauntless courage and willingness to bear responsibility, with a knowledge of men, and a far-reaching tact and kindliness, which enable his great abilities and high principles to be of use in a way that would be impossible were he not thus gifted with the capacity to work hand in hand with his fellows. President McKinley has rendered many great services to his country; and not the least has been the clear-sightedness with which he has chosen the best possible public servants to perform the very difficult tasks of acting as the first administrators in the islands

[14]

which came into our hands as a result of the Spanish war. Such was the service he rendered when he chose Assistant Secretary of the Navy Allen and afterwards Judge Hunt as Governors of Porto Rico; when he chose General Leonard Wood as Governor-General of Cuba; and finally when he made Judge Taft the first Governor of the Philippines.

When Judge Taft was sent out as the head of the Commission appointed by the President to inaugurate civil rule in the Philippines, he was in a position not only of great difficulty, but of great delicacy. He had to show inflexible strength, and yet capacity to work

[15]

heartily with other men and get the best results out of conflicting ideas and interests. The Tagalog insurrection was still under full headway, being kept alive largely by the moral aid it received from certain sources in this country. Any action of the Commission, no matter how wise and just, was certain to be misrepresented and bitterly attacked here at home by those who, from whatever reasons, desired the success of the insurgents. On the other hand, the regular army, which had done and was doing its work admirably — and which is entitled to the heartiest regard and respect from every true American, alive, as he should

[16]

be, to its literally inestimable services — was yet, from its very nature, not an instrument fitted for the further development of civil liberty in the islands. Under ordinary circumstances there would have been imminent danger of friction between the military and civil authorities. Fortunately, we had at the head of the War Department in Secretary Elihu Root a man as thoroughly fit for his post as Governor Taft was for his. Secretary Root was administering his department with an eye single to the public interests, his sole desire being to get the best possible results for the country. Where these results could be obtained by the

[17]

use of the army, he used it in the
most efficient possible manner —
and month by month, almost day
by day, its efficiency increased
under his hands. Where he thought
the best results could be obtained
by the gradual elimination of the
army and the substitution of civil
government, his sole concern was
to see that the substitution was
made in the most advantageous
manner possible. Neither the Secretary nor the Governor was capable of so much as understanding
the pettiness which makes a certain type of official, even in high
office, desire to keep official control
of some province of public work, not
for the sake of the public work, but

for the sake of the office. No better object-lesson could be given than has thus been given by Secretary Root and Governor Taft of the immense public benefit resulting, under circumstances of great difficulty and delicacy, from the cordial co-operation of two public servants, who combine entire disinterestedness with the highest standard of capacity.

Governor Taft thus set to work with the two great advantages of the hearty and generous support of his superior, the President, and the ungrudging coöperation of the War Department. The difficulties he had to combat were infinite. In the Philippines we were heirs to all

[19]

the troubles of Spain, and above all to the inveterate distrust and suspicion which Spanish rule had left in the native mind. The army alone could put down the insurrection, and yet, once the insurrection had been put down, every consideration of humanity and policy required that the function of the army should be minimized as much as possible. Until after the Presidential election in November last peace could not come, because both the insurgent leaders and their supporters on this side of the water were under the mistaken impression that a continuance of the bloodshed and struggle in the Philippines would be politically disadvanta-

[20]

geous to the party in power in the United States. Soon after the results of the election became known in the Philippines, however, armed resistance collapsed. The small bands now in the field are not, properly speaking, insurgents at all, but " ladrones," robbers whose operations are no more political than those of bandits in Calabria or Greece.

The way has thus been cleared for civil rule ; and astonishing progress has been made. Wherever possible, Governor Taft has been employing natives in the public service. Being a man of the soundest common sense, however, he has not hesitated to refuse to employ

natives where, after careful investigation, his deliberate judgment is
that, for the time being, it is to the
advantage of the natives themselves
that Americans should administer
the position, notably in certain of
the judgeships and high offices.
For the last few months the Filipinos have known a degree of peace,
justice, and prosperity to which
they have never attained in their
whole previous history, and to which
they could not have approximated
in the remotest degree had it not
been for the American stay in the
islands. Under Judge Taft they are
gradually learning what it means
to keep faith, what it means to have
public officials of unbending recti-

[22]

tude. Under him the islands have
seen the beginnings of a system of
good roads, good schools, upright
judges, and honest public servants.
His administration throughout has
been designed primarily for the
benefit of the islanders themselves,
and has therefore in the truest and
most effective way been in the interest also of the American Republic. Under him the islanders are
now taking the first steps along the
hard path which ultimately leads
to self-respect and self-government.
That they will travel this road with
success to the ultimate goal there
can be but little doubt, if only our
people will make it absolutely certain
that the policies inaugurated under

[23]

President McKinley by Governor
Taft shall be continued in the future
by just such men as Governor Taft.
There will be occasional failures, occasional shortcomings; and then we
shall hear the familiar wail of the
men of little faith, of little courage.
Here and there the smoldering
embers of insurrection will burst
again into brief flame; here and
there the measure of self-government granted to a given locality
will have to be withdrawn or dimin-
ished because on trial the people do
not show themselves fit for it; and
now and then we shall meet the
sudden and unexpected difficulties
which are inevitably incident to
any effort to do good to peoples

[24]

containing some savage and half-civilized elements. Governor Taft will have to meet crisis after crisis; he will meet each with courage, coolness, strength, and judgment.

It is highly important that we have good laws for the islands. It is highly important that these laws permit of the great material development of the islands. Governor Taft has most wisely insisted that it is to the immense benefit of the islanders that great industrial enterprises spring up in the Philippines, and of course such industrial enterprises can only spring up if profit comes to those who undertake them. The material uplifting of the people must go to-

moral monopoly

gether with their moral uplifting. But though it is important to have wise laws, it is more important that there should be a wise and honest administration of the laws. The statesmen at home, in Congress and out of Congress, can do their best work by following the advice and the lead of the man who is actually on the ground. It is therefore essential that this man should be of the very highest stamp. If inferior men are appointed, and, above all, if the curse of spoils politics ever fastens itself upon the administration of our insular dependencies, widespread disaster is sure to follow. Every American worthy of the name, every American who

[26]

is proud of his country and jealous of her honor, should uphold the hands of Governor Taft, and by the heartiness of his support should give an earnest of his intention to insist that the high standard set by Governor Taft shall be accepted for all time hereafter as the standard by which we intend to judge whoever, under or after Governor Taft, may carry forward the work he has so strikingly begun.

Governor Taft left a high office of honor and of comparative ease to undertake his present work. As soon as he became convinced where his duty lay he did not hesitate a moment, though he clearly foresaw the infinite labor, the crush-

[27]

ing responsibility, the certainty of recurring disappointments, and all the grinding wear and tear which such a task implies. But he gladly undertook it; and he is to be considered thrice fortunate! For in this world the one thing supremely worth having is the opportunity, coupled with the capacity, to do well and worthily a piece of work the doing of which is of vital consequence to the welfare of mankind.

CIVIL GOVERNMENT IN THE PHILIPPINES

BY WILLIAM H. TAFT

Civil Governor of the Philippines

CIVIL GOVERNMENT IN
THE PHILIPPINES

Firstnote

AS soon as the American army
extended its lines beyond the
city of Manila, and brought within
its control the various towns of the
islands, steps were taken by General Otis to inaugurate a simple
civil municipal government under
what were called Orders No. 43.
Thereafter, in the spring of 1900,
a commission appointed by General Otis reported a more extended
form of municipal government under General Orders No. 40. But
comparatively few towns were or-

ganized under Orders No. 40 before the Commission began to exercise its legislative jurisdiction in September, 1900. The civil branch of the military government under the Commanding General was a growth. He exercised both the legislative and executive power. He established civil courts in some six or eight of the provinces, generally appointing Filipinos to the bench. He appointed four judges of first instance in the city of Manila, and created a Supreme Court, following the organization of the Audiencia or Supreme Court as it existed under the Spaniards. This court he made up of both Americans and Filipinos, with Chief Justice Arellano, a Filipino, as its head. The secretary to the Military Governor was his chief assistant in carrying on the civil branch of his government, and the legislative work was done through his general orders or by the executive orders of the President. It was through one of the latter that the tariff act was put in force and duties collected under it. The customs office and the offices of the Treasurer and the Auditor of the islands were established. Under an executive order of the President and the appointment of the Postmaster-General, a post-office was organized and a Director-General of Posts began his duties. A Superinten-

[33]

dent of Schools for the city of Manila was appointed and some schools were opened there, first under Father McKinnon as Superintendent, and then under Mr. Anderson. The military government called into requisition the services of military officers by detailing them for civil duties. So much of the country was disturbed by the guerrilla war at the time that the operation of the civil branches of the government was exceedingly limited, and its expenses, by reason of the employment of detailed army officers who received no salaries from the civil funds, were not large. The customs receipts were considerable, and though a good deal of money was taken from the civil funds for purely military expenses, a satisfactory balance remained at the end of the fiscal year. The Commission in its problems was much aided by what had been done under the military government. From September, 1900, to July, 1901, the Commanding General of the Army was civil executive as well. This was a good arrangement, because it kept up the interest of the military branch in the development of the municipal governments until many could stand alone, and it enabled the Commission to secure through the Executive, during the transition from a military to a civil régime, the assistance of the army.

It was, however, no small task for the Commission first to enact legislation necessary to organize and establish the various bureaus and departments, and then to secure competent and faithful civilians to carry on the work of the central government, and to substitute them for military officers.

The fifth law which was enacted by the Commission was the civil service law, which is believed to extend the merit system further than it has ever been extended in this country. It is an indispensable condition precedent to any proper civil government in the islands; but it necessarily imposed restrictions in the selection of employees, which have, in some cases, delayed the organization of offices.

The first act passed by the Commission appropriated one million dollars for the construction and improvement of roads in the Archipelago. Another early act of the Commission provided for the improvement of the harbor works of Manila, and involved an expenditure of three millions of dollars. I shall not dwell upon the necessity for the construction of roads in the Philippines. In no other respect are the islands so backward as in the lack of intercommunication between the towns of the interior.

[37]

The harbor of Manila at present is not at all satisfactory. A popular impression exists that Manila Bay is small enough to form a harbor in itself, but this is a great mistake. The bay is thirty-five miles long by twenty-five miles wide, and opposite to Manila is the opening between the China Sea and the bay, sufficiently wide to give free sweep to the southwest monsoon, so that during the wet season, when that monsoon prevails, vessels anchored in the Bay of Manila find it very difficult to load or unload. The Spaniards built part of a breakwater, but very little protection was thus given to shipping. The Pasig River offers a harbor for vessels of sixteen feet draft, but it is so crowded that the demand for more harbor room is imperative. It is hoped that the harbor work will be completed in two years, and, with a good harbor and a reduction of landing charges, the port of Manila will undoubtedly become one of the most important in the Orient.

Between September, 1900, and January, 1901, the Commission enacted other legislation looking toward the better organization of the central government bureaus and departments. It had also in preparation the acts providing for the creation of municipal and provincial governments; but until the election of President McKinley gave the people of the islands to understand what the policy of the United States was to be, the Commission did not deem it wise to attempt to carry out its plans for partial self-government of the islands. In December, 1900, and January and February of 1901, full discussion was held at the public sessions of the Commission in respect to the provisions of these important organizing acts, and they were made into law in February of that year. The municipal law is drawn on the same general plan as the municipal codes of this country, and the government is practically autonomous. The electorate is limited to those who speak and write either Spanish or English, those who pay a tax of fifteen dollars a year, or to those who have filled municipal offices. The provincial government is partially autonomous. The office of Governor is elective. The Governor is a member of the provincial legislative board. His colleagues on this board are the Treasurer and Supervisor, who are appointed under the civil service law. The Governor and Treasurer exercise supervision over the municipal officers of their province. Thus far they have been Americans. The other provincial officers are the Prosecuting Attorney or Fiscal, and the Secretary. They have been Filipinos. The

Secretary is now selected under the civil service law. The Commission, which is the legislative body of the central government since the first of September, 1901, has five American members and three Filipino members, appointed by the President.

Conditions improved so rapidly after the beginning of 1901 that the Commission felt justified in visiting various provinces to organize provincial governments. Four months of the time between February, 1901, and September, 1901, was taken up in establishing thirty-four provincial governments. Of these, thirty-three were in provinces in which there were none but Christian Filipinos. One, the province of Benguet, in the mountains, contained only Igorrotes or hill tribes. The government of Benguet was, therefore, of the most paternal character and left most of the power, either by direct intervention or supervision, with the Governor. To the other provinces — the Christian Filipino provinces — the general provincial law was made applicable by special acts which were passed after a conference with the leading men of the province, and contained provisions varying the general provincial act to suit differing local conditions.

[43]

Between the first of January and the first of September, 1901, the Commission passed a general school law, and under this the Superintendent of Public Instruction, Mr. Atkinson, brought to the islands about one thousand American schoolteachers. The teachers did not reach the islands before August, and were not assigned and transported to their posts much before the first of October. There are about nine hundred towns in the Archipelago, and these teachers were sent to about five hundred of them. In addition to the thousand American school-teachers there are about twenty-five hundred Filipino school-teachers. The chief function of the American school-teacher is to teach the Filipino teacher English, and proper methods of teaching. The American school-teachers do, of course, teach in the primary schools, but the plan is that the teaching of the Filipino children shall chiefly be done by Filipino teachers. Normal schools have been organized in the islands, and manual training schools. The immense amount of detail required, not only for the establishment of schools, but for the furnishing of a commissary for the school-teachers, will be understood only by those who know the difficulties of transportation and communication between Manila and the towns of the islands. Among the thousand school-teachers it is not surprising that some should be found disposed to complain of the system which is being inaugurated. The school system as a system has really been in operation for not more than six months. It would be entirely unjust and foolish, after so short a time, to render a final judgment as to the wisdom of the system, were it being inaugurated in a country as well adapted to receive a school system as the United States. Still more unwise and unjust is it to attempt to reach a final conclusion as to its successful operation or otherwise when a system of this kind is applied to a country with such unusual conditions as those prevailing in the Philippine Islands. Not for five years will it be fair to speak with confidence of the effect and the efficiency of the school system in the Philippines. Certainly, neither the Commission nor the Superintendent is likely to be driven from a policy inaugurated after as full an investigation as could be made, by the grumblings and criticisms of employees assigned to provinces not so important as they think their abilities and capacities require.

The exact attitude of the Catholic Church to the schools has not been clearly defined. It is quite probable that this will not be the

[47]

same in some provinces as in others. It is known to vary in this country, according to the views of the priesthood in the particular locality, and the same thing will be true in the Philippines. The Commission has not the slightest objection to the spread of church schools, if only a proper standard of education is maintained in them; on the contrary, it welcomes any aid in education. It may be necessary to pass a compulsory education law when the school system shall be sufficiently enlarged to offer to all children of school age an opportunity for education. At present the difficulty of providing schools for those who are willing to attend is

so great that compulsory attendance would seem to be unreason-
able. However, it should be said
that the Commission is constantly
in receipt of petitions from the various towns of the Archipelago ask-
ing that a compulsory education
law be passed. In such a case, of
course, attendance at church schools
would satisfy the law, provided a
curriculum was maintained cover-
ing certain required subjects. It is
very important that English be
taught in all the schools, in order
that the next generation shall have
a common medium of communication. The Filipinos have very considerable facility in learning languages, and are very anxious to

learn English. A knowledge of English, and a consequent familiarity with American literature and American newspapers, will furnish to the people a means of understanding American civilization and American institutions, and will greatly assist in teaching them self-government on Anglo-Saxon lines. One necessary addition to the school system is the establishment of schools of secondary instruction, and probably a university. The primary schools teach English. There are some Filipinos in each town, however, who will desire their children to have an academic education, and unless we furnish secondary schools, in which English shall be the language taught, we shall disappoint the legitimate ambition and aspiration of such parents. In other words, a primary system in English requires a secondary and probably university instruction in the same language.

The step next most important to the beginning of a school system in the islands has been the organization of a judiciary. An impartial administration of justice is what has been most lacking in Philippine civilization, and the Commission has thought it wise that a judiciary should be established in which American judges should be in the majority. The whole Archipelago has been divided into fifteen judicial districts, in each of which there is a court of first instance with a general civil and criminal jurisdiction like that of the ordinary common pleas court in this country. A justice of the peace with jurisdiction like that of our justices of the peace is appointed in each town, and appeal from his decision to the courts of first instance is provided. A Supreme Court of seven members, with appellate jurisdiction over the judgments of the courts of first instance, has been created to sit at Manila, Iloilo, and Cebú. In the Supreme Court four Americans and three Filipinos sit, and about one third of the judges of first instance are Filipinos. In the large cities, in which there is likely to be litigation between foreigners or Americans and Filipinos, American judges have usually been selected. This is done in order to avoid the necessity for a so-called United States Court to which Americans and foreigners may carry their cases. As much care as possible has been used in the selection of the judges, and I feel confident that we have inaugurated a system in which justice will be done, and the inestimable benefit will be conferred upon the people of showing them what justice is. We have certainly succeeded in securing the "pick" of the Filipino lawyers for the bench, and the American judges have shown themselves to be men thoroughly in earnest in their work and greatly interested in maintaining a high standard for the courts.

As an aid in the administration of justice and the maintenance of law and order, in addition to the local police, it has been necessary to establish an insular constabulary. This consists of not more than one hundred and fifty men in each province, under inspectors partly American and partly Filipino. Ladronism was very widely extended under the Spanish rule, and there was organized under the government what was called the guardia civil, but the outrages and abuses of the guardia civil were almost equal to those committed by the ladrones. I am glad to say that thus far the operation of the constabulary system has been most satisfactory, and ladronism is rapidly disappearing. The selection of men for its ranks has been very carefully made. The system of selecting only residents of the province for service in the province avoids the danger of abuse and looting by the members of the constabulary themselves. In a force of some five thousand men there have been reported but three desertions. The constabulary costs the

Philippine Government $250 a man a year, on the average.

During the period between January and September of 1901 the Commission adopted, with the assistance of the War Department, a new tariff which reversed the principle of the Spanish tariff by imposing a higher duty upon luxuries than upon necessaries, and by reducing the duty upon foodstuffs, canned goods, and other necessaries, from a prohibitory rate to an ad valorem tax of about fifteen per cent. The average rate of the whole tariff schedule is an ad valorem duty of from twenty-five to thirty per cent. The customs department had to be reorganized, and a customs administrative bill was passed in November, 1900, adopting largely the American system of appraisement and collection.

The Bureau of Forestry, which has under its protection one of the largest sources of wealth in the islands, in the last year has been much extended and more completely organized, so that it now has its agents in every province of the islllands to collect the timber license fees and to see to it that the forests are not injured by the cutting permitted.

The Post-Office is being extended gradually, but it is not by any means as efficient as it ought to be.

The difficulties of communication are very great. The Commission has contracted for the construction of twenty small sea-going vessels with which it is hoped that the mails can be carried and a revenue police system maintained, and that the provincial officials may be transported between the various towns of their province, and that frequent communication may thus be had between the capitals of provinces and Manila. But these vessels will not all be ready for service before next year. Under the present system it sometimes takes more time to reach the capitals of some of the more remote provinces from Manila than it does to go to San Francisco.

The Commission has organized a complete health department under the central government, which co-operates with local health officials. This is essential both in the protection of the people of the islands from epidemics of smallpox, cholera, and plague, and in stamping out contagious diseases of cattle and horses. A very heavy expense has been thrown upon the central government in its attempts to keep the cholera now existing in the islands from spreading.

An agricultural bureau has been organized, the importance of which in developing proper methods of agriculture in these islands, and superseding the uselessly clumsy manner in which crops are sown and reaped, cannot be overstated. Some of the most expert scientists of the Agricultural Department of Washington have been brought to the islands, and it is hoped that in the course of three or four years marked improvement in agricultural methods may be made through the instrumentality of model farms and direct instruction in agricultural schools.

Until Congress acts, the survey and sale of public lands and mining rights will probably be held in abeyance, but as the bill for the civil government of the Philippines is likely to pass before the close of this session of Congress, it is certain that these two bureaus must be very much enlarged. Of course a very comprehensive and extensive system of surveys is absolutely necessary to the proper application of any public land or public mining system, and this will have to be begun at once. The civil government is almost wholly dependent on receipts from customs for its income.

It will be a serious question whether the government as planned can be carried on without a deficit if business and the revenues do not increase. If the revenues do not increase, it will be necessary for the Commission to economize by delaying the execution of some of its plans and by radical retrenchment. The

cost of the school system is heavy,
and in all probability will increase.
The necessity for more teachers and
the erection of permanent school
buildings is immediate.

I think I have outlined the plans
of the Commission with respect to
the central government bureaus sufficiently to show that a good deal
of money will be needed to carry
them out. In addition to what I
have said, the Philippine Government ought to make a comprehensive exhibit at the Louisiana
Purchase Exposition to be held at
St. Louis in 1904, and it was hoped
that half a million dollars might be
appropriated for this purpose ; but

the Commission has decided that it cannot enter into an obligation to pay out that much money until further time has been given to determine what the income-producing capacity of the present tariff law is.

The work of the Commission has been hard and exacting. The difficulty of selecting competent officers to act as heads of bureaus and departments eight thousand miles away from the United States will be appreciated. The difficulty of selecting Filipinos for important offices where faction and prejudice and personal ambition play a very decided part can be understood. The great labor needed in the preparation of the laws, an examination of

[63]

the acts of the Commission will
show. One of the heaviest labors
has been the preparation and enactment of a code of civil procedure.
The code follows generally the codes
of the American States. The Spanish code of procedure was so full of
technicalities as practically to deny
justice to the litigant, and the Filipino bar were unanimous in a demand for a change. Judge Ide has
drafted the code, and I believe that
American lawyers who consult it
will testify to the excellence of his
work. The old Spanish criminal
code was continued by General Otis,
with necessary modifications, as
well as the criminal code of practice. A new code of practice and

of crimes has now been prepared by
General Wright, and only awaits
enactment when the three lawyers
of the Commission can meet to-
gether again. The Commission,
under its instructions, has not attempted to change the substantive
law of the islands so far as it affects
the correlative rights and duties of
individuals. It is the civil law,
and does not differ very materially
from the Code Napoleon. It is a
good system of law, and there is no
reason to change it.

When the tariff bill enacted into
law by Congress was before the
Senate, there was severe criticism
of the Commission for passing what

were known as the treason and sedition laws. So far as this criticism related to sections which were taken bodily from the Revised Statutes of the United States, and had been in those statutes for one hundred years, I hardly think it necessary to say anything. A section was taken from the Spanish laws which in effect, though not in language, was like a section of the United States Revised Statutes providing for the punishment of conspiracy on the part of two or more persons to deprive another of rights secured to him by the Constitution of the United States. Another section of the act was almost a literal copy of a Tennessee statute denouncing sedition. Another section forbade the organization of secret political societies, and another forbade the advocacy of independence pending the war either by peaceable or by forcible means. The latter section was by its terms merely a war measure, and to a certain extent suspended free speech. As peace is now likely to be officially declared at any time, it hardly needs further comment than to say that it was enacted, not to prevent the sincere advocacy of independence by peaceable means, though it had such an effect temporarily, but really to prevent the encouragement of men in arms against the sovereignty of the

United States, by an advocacy of independence, either with no limitation or with a mere pretense of limiting the advocacy to peaceable means. Members of the Insurgent Junta began to move toward Manila, with the apparent impression that the establishment of civil government in Manila would allow them free scope for their political agitation. The section denouncing secret political societies was adopted for the same purpose as the section just discussed, and, while not expressly limited to the pendency of war, may be regarded as war legislation. The section against sedition was, as I have said, copied from a Tennessee statute, and was

[68]

intended to secure the public welfare against articles intended to disturb the peace by gross libels upon the government or upon any class of people. There is nothing in the privilege of free speech or a free press that renders immune from prosecution those guilty of misrepresentation or libel. The conditions prevailing in the Philippines make the passage of such a law necessary. There are in the city of Manila American papers owned and edited by Americans who have the bitterest feeling toward the Filipinos, and entertain the view that legislation for the benefit of the Filipinos or appointment to office of Filipinos is evidence of a lack of loyalty to the Americans who have come to settle in the islands. Accordingly, they write the most scurrilous articles impeaching the honesty of the Filipino officials, the Filipino judges, and the whole Filipino people, as a basis for attacking the policy of the Commission. The editor of the " Freedom " has been prosecuted under this section for publishing an article which is described by General Wright, the Acting Civil Governor of the Philippine Islands, as follows:

The editor of the " Freedom " has been proceeded against on account of a lengthy editorial attacking civil government in general and Filipino people in particular, charging that Commission constitute a protectorate over set of men who should be in jail or deported, that they were all knaves and hypocrites. Referred to Valdes libel as showing Tavera coward and rascal, Legarda unworthy to associate with respectable people, and attacked American Commissioners for recommending them and permitting them remain members. Charges Filipino judiciary notoriously corrupt and unwilling to convict Filipinos. Denominate all Filipino officials rascally natives, rogues, notoriously corrupt and men of no character. Manifest purpose to stir up race hatred and especially make odious and contemptible Filipino members of Commission and Filipino officials generally, and create breach between Filipinos and Americans, thereby disturbing the peace of the community.

[71]

In a country like the United States such an article would not cause any particular trouble, but in the Philippines it is at once translated into Spanish and into Tagalog and is used for the purpose of stirring up race hatred; and this was probably the purpose for which it was written. The paper in which the article appeared has always advocated great severity in dealing with the Filipinos, and has done everything to avoid the establishment of good feeling which ought to exist between the Filipino people and those Americans who are in the islands. The editor of the "Freedom" has the opportunity to prove, if he can, in his defense, the corruption which he charges, but if it turns out that his charges are unfounded, I think he ought to be punished, and that his punishment will not be in violation of any right to free speech. In a country like the United States it is wiser not to denounce many acts as offenses against the law which might properly be denounced as such, because their evil effect is negligible in this community; but such acts in a country like the Philippines, under the peculiar conditions there prevailing, may be exceedingly injurious to the public peace, and may properly call for a statutory denunciation of them without impairing any of the rights described in the bill of rights.

The people of the Archipelago are divided roughly into six and one half million Christian Filipinos, one million and a half Moros or Mohammedans, and one million other non-Christian tribes, known usually as hill tribes. The insurrection has been maintained only by the Christian Filipinos. Neither the hill tribes nor the Moros took any part in it. The Christian Filipinos are the only people of the islands who have the slightest conception of popular government.

The present condition of the Christian Filipino provinces is that of peace. When I left the islands in December, 1901, there was insurrection only in the provinces of

[74]

Batangas, Laguna, Samar, Tayabas, and some little in Mindoro. It was also claimed that there was some insurrection in the province of Misamis, though it seemed to me that it was more of a ladrone disturbance than one of the insurrectos. However that may be, the fact is now that all forces in arms in Batangas, Tayabas, Laguna, Samar, Mindoro, and Misamis have surrendered, and their rifles have been delivered up to the military authorities. These provinces are ripe for the establishment of civil government, and it is probable that within two months the provincial governments in those provinces will have been estab-

[75]

lished.[1] When this is done, all
the Christian Filipino provinces to
which the provincial law can be
practically applied will enjoy peace
and civil government. There are
two provinces on the Pacific coast
known as Infanta and Principe, in
which the population does not exceed ten or fifteen thousand, which
are so sparsely settled that a special
form of government must be given
them, and the same thing is true
of the Calamianes group in the Jolo
Sea. There are ladrones in the

---

[1] On July 4, 1902, less than two months from the
time when this was written, President Roosevelt
was able to proclaim that civil government was
established everywhere in the Philippines except
in the territory occupied by the Moros, and to
issue also a proclamation of general amnesty.—
THE PUBLISHERS.

province of Leyte who are being rapidly dispersed, captured, or killed by the constabulary, and the same thing is true of Negros. In Negros there never has been insurrection, but the impassable mountains and forests which form the spine of the island have always offered refuge to a mountain people who have made a profession of cattle-lifting and blackmailing. The rich hacienda-owners of the plains of eastern and western Negros have always suffered from this evil. It is the purpose of the Commission to eradicate it, but the ladrones are so numerous and the difficulties of campaigning so great that it will take a considerable time.

The difficulty with the Lake Lanao Moros, the wild Moros of Mindanao, has no more to do with the insurrection than did Indian fights on the plains or in Minnesota have to do with the Civil War. With the establishment of civil government in the near future, therefore, over all the six million of Christian Filipinos, the difficulties inherent in the dual form of control by the military and the civil authorities will be eliminated. The army will be concentrated in a comparatively few garrisoned posts separated from the towns, and stricter discipline will be much easier to maintain when the troops cease to be quartered on the people. When the troops are withdrawn to separate posts and the

people see them but occasionally,
they will be much more convinced
of the real power of civil government and much more satisfied of the
benevolent intentions of the American authorities. Under orders
which have now been issued by the
War Department, the American
troops will be reduced to a force
of eighteen thousand men as soon
as the Government transports can
comply with the orders.

There has been a general tendency
among the military officers to regard civil government as a failure,
and this view has been reflected
by those correspondents who have
been with the army and have im-

bibed the opinion of the army messes and the Army and Navy Club in Manila; but a better acquaintance with the actual governments shows these criticisms to be unfounded. The civil provincial governments and the municipal governments are going concerns, having defects in their operation it is true, but nevertheless furnishing to the people who are subject to their respective jurisdictions a protection to life, liberty, and property, an opportunity to obtain justice through the courts, education for their children in the schools, and the right to pursue their usual vocations. The suggestion that in the so-called pacified provinces insurrection is

still seething is wholly unfounded.
The people are engaged in their ordinary occupations, and while they
have been much injured by the loss
of their cattle through the rinder-
pest, they are struggling with this
difficulty and are raising rice in sufficient quantities to avoid a famine.
An examination of the annual reports of the governors of the different provinces contained in the
printed evidence before the Senate
Committee will support this statement. Taxes are being collected
in the provinces, the processes of
the court run without obstruction,
and the February elections of governors were held without disturbance, and, on the whole, satisfac-

tory candidates were selected. The Christian Filipino people are now enjoying greater individual liberty and a greater voice in their government than ever before in their history, and with the official declaration of peace now near at hand, both will be increased. Much has been said in the heat of debate and of partisan journalism concerning the feeling of hatred of the Filipinos toward the Americans. So far as the civil government is concerned, no such feeling exists. The Commission visited forty provinces and districts of the islands in the period between the first of February and the first of September, 1901, and occupied in all about four months in its trip. The receptions given it by the educated and ignorant people alike, and the enthusiastic welcome which it received, all convinced the Commission that the people were friendly to civil government and earnestly desired its establishment. They have taken great interest in the civil government since, and nothing has occurred to change the deep impression made upon the Commission by the good feeling manifested and expressions of gratitude received on this trip.

The feeling of the people toward the army is different. In some places it is friendly and in others it is hostile, and it is found chiefly to vary with the disposition of the commanding officer of the post in the neighborhood. If he be abrupt, arbitrary, and surly in his treatment of the people, they do not like him. If he is interested in their welfare, is kindly and polite in dealing with them, they do like him. Toward the civil government, however, which has always followed the policy of "attraction," as it is called in the islands, in dealing with the people, their attitude is an entirely friendly one. It is quite natural that it should be. It was through the coming of the Civil Commission that the rigor of military rule was softened and removed. It is through frequent intercession of the civil authorities that military prisoners have been released, and the people are well aware that in the conflicts of jurisdiction between the civil government and the military government, of which there have been a number, the civil government was seeking to save the Filipinos from military arrest and prosecution.

It is too much to say that the Commission has done all that can be done under its present powers, because doubtless there is much in the way of perfecting the present provincial and municipal governments that could occupy its time

[85]

and attention profitably; but it is true that the time has now come when improvement in present conditions can be best brought about by the passage of a bill by Congress for the government of the Philippine Islands.[1] There are two bills pending — one in the Senate and one in the House. Both bills embody the wise policy of not disturbing the present system of government, which has proved satisfactory. The principle has been followed, so

[1] Since this was written, Congress has passed, and the President has signed, a Philippine Act which agrees in many points with the suggestions here made by Governor Taft, but differs in some particulars. A popular legislative assembly is to be organized two years after a census provided for by the act is taken; the only restriction on the suffrage in the election of members is that the

well established in Anglo-Saxon government-building, of taking what is in existence and improving and adding to it. The Senate bill differs from the House bill, however, in several material respects. The House bill provides that after peace shall be declared, and after a census shall have been taken, the Commission shall call a general election for the selection of representatives to form a popular assembly, which shall constitute one branch

voters must be either property-owners or able to speak Spanish or English. The matter of coinage is left untouched by the act, so that the present laws continue in force. The act provides for grants of public lands to corporations, but not over twenty-five hundred acres can be granted to one corporation, and there are other restrictions upon the grants.—THE PUBLISHERS.

[87]

of the legislature of the islands, the Commission to constitute the other branch. The House bill further provides for the selection by the popular assembly and the Commission of two delegates who shall represent their constituents before the executive and legislative branches of the Government at Washington. The House bill provides for the establishment of a gold standard of value in the islands, to wit, the American gold dollar. It further provides for the coinage of a Filipino peso to contain silver of value in gold of about forty cents or less, and a useful and proper subsidiary coinage. This coinage is to be limited to the government only, and the seignior-

age is reserved as a fund to maintain the parity of the peso with fifty
cents gold.   Other means are provided in the act by which the Philippine Government is authorized to
maintain the parity.   It is hoped
by the Commission that recommended this plan, and by the Committee of the House, that it will
prevent the fluctuations of value
due to the use of Mexican currency,
and will at the same time furnish
a coinage so near to the present
coinage as not to create a disturbance in values or in wages.   The
Senate bill does not provide for a
legislative assembly or the appointment of the two delegates, nor does
it make provision for a gold stan-

[89]

dard. In place of these it directs the taking of a census after peace shall be declared, and the recommendation by the Commission of the form of government to be permanently established. It provides also for the free coinage of a Filipino dollar of the size and weight of the Mexican dollar, which it is hoped will become a well-known coin in the commerce of the East.

We of the Commission are very earnest and sincere in our hope that at least the provision for the election of the legislative assembly and of the two delegates contained in the House bill shall be embodied in legislation. We think that the

Filipino people would accept this provision as the most indubitable evidence of the desire of the United States that self-government should be given to the people in as large a measure as they are capable of carrying it on. Danger from obstruction of the government by withholding supplies is avoided in a section of the House bill by a provision that, should the appropriation bill not be passed, appropriations equal to those of the year before shall become available without legislation. There are members of the Senate Committee on the Philippines who believe that the step involved in the organization of a legislative assembly is too pro-

gressive and too radical. In this
I think they are mistaken. It is
quite possible that on the floor of
the legislative assembly will be pro-
claimed doctrines at variance with
the policy of the United States, and
that possibly, by some members,
seditious and treasonable speeches
may be made; but, on the whole,
I feel sure that the people will regard the legislative assembly as a
welcome method by which they can
take part in the government, and
that there will be every disposition
on the part of most of the members
to work harmoniously with the
other branch of the legislative department and with the Executive.
It has been suggested that possibly

the legislative assembly would se-
lect Aguinaldo or Mabini or some
other prominent insurrecto leader
or organizer to represent it at
Washington. I do not think this
is likely; but even if it were to
happen, I should not regard it as a
dangerous result. I think it would
be found that the popular assembly
would include many conservative
men who would be in favor of supporting American sovereignty in
the islands and making the government it has established firm and
stable. A provision of this kind
would destroy at once the suspi-
cions of American good faith, and
would largely satisfy the desire for
self-government of all but the com-

[93]

paratively few irreconcilables. A popular assembly would be a great educational school for the better class of Filipinos in actual government. The weakness of the educated Filipinos to-day is in their lack of practical knowledge as to how a popular government ought to be run. They always resort to absolutism in practical problems of government. The restrictions upon the suffrage contained in the municipal code, which are by reference made part of the House bill, would secure a fairly intelligent body of representatives in the popular assembly.

The result of the popular assembly in the Hawaiian Islands has been referred to as a warning against the extension of such privileges in the Philippines; but it must be noted that the difficulty in the Hawaiian Islands resulted not so much from the establishment of a popular assembly as from the undue extension of the electoral franchise. In the Philippines the franchise has been restricted and duly guarded.

I am not blind to the troubles that the legislative assembly would doubtless bring to the Executive and to the Commission in rousing public discussion over unimportant matters which now perhaps pass without notice; but I am not at all sure that such public discussion would not, on the whole, work for

[95]

the public welfare. The fact that a vote of the Commission would be necessary to the enactment of any law is quite a sufficient veto for practical purposes. Should the legislative assembly feature, which the Federal party has petitioned for, which the Commission has recommended, and which the Committee of the House has recommended, be eliminated, it will cause very serious disappointment to the Filipino people.

The agricultural and commercial communities in the Philippines are anxious that the Dingley tariff rates against products of the islands should be reduced. The rates are now reduced in favor of Philippine

importations twenty-five per cent.,
but the Commission is convinced
that the reduction should be seventy-five per cent., and that with
such a reduction the commerce
between the Philippines and the
United States will gradually increase to a very large volume. I
think it is recognized by members of Congress, both in the
Senate and in the House, that this
reduction of twenty-five per cent.
is only the beginning, and that
the tendency must necessarily be
toward free trade. We do not
seek absolute free trade, because
tariffs should be reciprocal, and an
ad valorem duty of twenty-five per
cent. on imports from the United

[97]

States to the Philippines seems necessary to furnish the needed revenues to the islands. We sincerely hope that next session will see a further material reduction, and that within a measurably short time at least a seventy-five per cent. reduction will be made. What the Filipino people long for is expressions of good will from the Americans, and nothing would be more welcome than this invitation to come into the American markets.

The House bill differs from the Senate bill also in containing a declaration or bill of rights in favor of the Filipino people under the government by the bill established. It secures all the rights declared in the bill of rights and the Constitution of the United States, except the right to bear arms and the right of trial by jury. Any one familiar with Filipino civilization will understand the wisdom of withholding from the Filipino people the enjoyment of these two privileges. If arms could be purchased without restriction, ladronism in the islands would be widely extended, and the maintenance of law and order most difficult. The bearing of arms may not be safely enjoyed by the Filipino people until the great mass of them shall have acquired more self-restraint than can now be found among them; nor can the jury system be safely put in practice now, even among those who are qualified to vote. The Commission has provided for the selection of two assessors of fact to assist the judges in reaching conclusions on issues of fact; but the great majority of the electorate, even limited as it is, are not now fitted to take part in the administration of justice and reach conclusions free from prejudice and bias or danger of corruption. The House bill further declares that a resident of the Philippine Islands owing allegiance to the United States shall enjoy the same protection from injury by foreign governments or

in foreign countries as citizens of
the United States. It is wise to
spread these declarations of rights
in favor of the Filipinos upon the
face of the statute which gives
them a voice in their own government, and I am sure it will have a
good effect in making them understand the intention of the Government of the United States.

Both bills empower the legislature
of the islands to grant franchises
for the building of commercial and
street railroads and for the formation of corporations for other purposes. Both bills limit the power
of acquisition of land by a corporation, foreign or domestic, to five

[101]

thousand acres. It seems to me that this limitation is too low, and that it ought to be raised to twenty thousand acres, for the reason that, in order to attract capital and to induce agricultural development on the best lines, especially in the production of sugar and tobacco, the cultivation must be of estates at least as large as fifteen or twenty thousand acres. This is the size of estates in Cuba and in the Sandwich Islands. There are only five millions of acres held by individuals in the islands, while the public lands probably exceed sixty-five millions of acres in extent. I have no desire to promote such an exploitation of the islands as will

center ownership of the interests
there in a few individuals, but it
seems to me that it is most unwise
to impose such restrictions as are
likely either to prevent the coming
of capital at all or to lead to unlaw-
ful and fraudulent evasions of the
restrictions. The cost of a modern
sugar-plant is very heavy, and cap-
italists cannot be induced to make
the investment unless the extent of
the land to be cultivated by them
and the probable production are sufficient to warrant the necessarily
large outlay. The investment of
American capital in the islands is
necessary to their proper development, and is necessary to the material, and therefore the spiritual,

uplifting of the Filipino people. It means the construction of railroads, the needed intercommunication between the people and the provinces, and a change from a comparatively poor and ignorant people to one of comparative intelligence and wealth.

The question is frequently asked why it would not be well to promise the Filipino people that, when they are fitted for complete self-government, they shall be granted independence. In the first place, the Federal party, which furnishes the only organized expression of public opinion in the islands, does not ask independence, but seeks rather annexation to the United

States and prospective Statehood. In the second place, there is not the slightest probability that the Christian Filipinos will be ready for self-government in any period short of two generations. Not ten per cent. of the people speak Spanish, and the remaining ninety per cent. or more are densely ignorant, superstitious, and subject to imposition of all sorts. It is absolutely necessary, in order that the people be taught self-government, that a firm, stable government under American guidance and control, in which the Filipino people shall have a voice, should be established. Nothing but such a government can educate the people into a knowledge of what self-government is. Not only by precept but by practice must the self-restraints essential to self-government and the discretion and public spirit of a free people be taught them. A promise to give the people independence when they are fitted for it would inevitably be accepted by the agitators and generally by the people as a promise to give them independence within the present generation, and would therefore be misleading, and the source of bitter criticism of the American government within a few years after the promise was given and not performed as it was understood by the people. A promise of independence thus interpreted

would destroy the possibility of the
formation of a stable government
in which the people should be learning what self-government is, because the conservative element, with
the assumed early prospect of complete independence, would fear that
when the islands were abandoned
the violent agitators would come to
the front, and those assisting the
present government would be subjected to the hostility of the dema-
gogues on the ground of their previous American sympathies. The
only policy, it seems to me, which
will insure the establishment of a
firm, stable government, and the
support of that government by the
educated, wealthy, and conservative

Filipinos, is the declaration of a policy in favor of the indefinite retention of the islands under a government in which the share taken by the Filipino people shall be made gradually to increase and the electorate of the Filipino people shall be gradually enlarged. After this government shall be successfully established, the question whether the islands shall be annexed or shall be granted independence, or shall have such a relation to this country as Australia or Canada has to England, may be very well postponed until the practical education of the people in self-government shall have been sufficient to justify the adoption of either of these three courses. The policy of establishing a firm and stable government in which the Filipino people shall take part will doubtless reveal much as to the wisdom of the one or the other of the courses suggested; but it seems to me to be very unwise to bind ourselves and the next generation by an authoritative declaration now as to what we shall do fifty or a hundred years hence. We cannot now know what subsequent generations of our own people will then deem wise, or what succeeding generations of Filipinos, benefited by experience in self-government and advised of the advantage of association with the United States, will desire.

The opponents of the Administration policy in the Philippines do not agree with one another. If I have correctly understood Senator Rawlins, of the minority of the Senate Committee on the Philippines, in his questions put me when before the Senate Committee, he believes that the best thing for the Government to do is to turn over the islands to a strong man who shall maintain absolute rule over the people with no popular voice in the government. His view is that in Oriental countries no other than the absolute rule of a strong man is possible. If this be the true view, then hope of securing individual liberty to the people of the

Philippines must be abandoned, and the policy of those gentlemen who, like Senator Hoar, entertain the idea that by leaving the islands it will be possible to form a Filipino Republic in which all the rights of individual liberty will be secured to the Filipinos must be given up. President Schurman, after six months' observation of the people, reached the conclusion that they would not be fit for self-government short of a generation or longer. He now has reached the opinion, based on the reports of the present United States Philippine Commission and the observations of General Chaffee in reviewing criminal cases, that he was wrong in his judgment, and

[111]

that the Filipino people will be capable of self-government after six or eight years of American tutelage, and this though the gentlemen upon whose statements he relies for his change of view agree with his former conclusion. The theory of President Schurman seems to be that the independence of a government and the individual liberty of its subjects or citizens are the same thing, or at least that the one is essential to the other.

This, it seems to me, involves a radical error. Whether independence will aid in securing individual liberty depends on the fitness for popular self-government of the people. If they are ignorant and

easily led, then independence means
ultimately absolutism and not liberty. The independence under
present conditions of the Philippine
Islands will mean the subjection
and not the liberty of the people.
It will mean internecine warfare
and will be followed by such an absolute government as that which
Senator Rawlins seems to think
best for them.

The minority in the Philippines
Committee in the Senate propose a
constitutional convention within a
year from the passage of the act,
the delegates to which are to be
selected by the votes of all the
adult males of the Archipelago who
can read and write. There are the

million and a half Moros in Mindanao and the Jolo group, and the
million or more of the hill tribes-
men. Why, under the theories of
the minority, should the Moros or
hill tribes be subjected to the rule
of the Christian Filipinos, whom
they dislike, and whose government they would certainly resist?
The Democratic minority of the
House Committee, with what seems
to me greater judgment, proposes
the establishment of a government
in which there shall be some American supervision and guidance for
six or eight years. They expressly
recognize the fact that three hundred years of Spanish rule have not
been calculated to fit the people of

the Philippine Islands for self-
government; but the assumption
that six years of a government
under American guidance will ac-
complish such a result seems to me
only less reasonable than the pro-
posal of the Democratic minority
in the Senate. No account is taken
in these plans of the peculiar traits
of the Moro population, of the den-
sity of ignorance of ninety per cent.
of the Christian Filipino population,
or of the utterly uncivilized condition of the hill tribes. The difficulty that the opponents of the
Administration have in finding a
common affirmative policy to uphold is an indication of the correct-
ness of the Administration plan, to

[115]

wit : that of the establishment of a firm and stable government now for the Christian Filipinos, with as much share in the government as they can safely exercise, without any definite declaration as to what may be done in the far-distant future; and separate forms of paternal government for the Moros and the other non-Christian tribes.

The insurrection in the Philippines is at an end, but the difficulties of civil government are by no means ended. The first difficulty has already been alluded to. It consists in the possible inadequacy of the revenues of the islands to meet the expenses of much-needed works of reform

and improvement in the Archipelago. The expenses of the government are increased by the necessity for the employment of many
Americans and for paying them
adequate compensation. To secure
good work in the Philippines from
Americans higher salaries must be
paid than in the United States.
The grave mistake in the Spanish
administration of the Archipelago
was in the payment of very low
salaries to their officials, who took
this as a justification for illegal ex-
actions from the people. It is
hoped, however, that with the ex-
pected increase in business and
commerce due to the investment of
capital in the islands, revenues may

increase and permit a proper expansion of government agencies in the development of the Archipelago.

The second difficulty which confronts the civil government is to be found in the questions which grow out of the former relation of the Roman Catholic Church to the Spanish government in the islands. Under the Spanish rule the property and political interests of the government were so inextricably confused with those of the Church that now, when, under the Treaty of Paris, the interests of the Spanish government have been transferred to the United States, which

by a law of its being cannot
continue the partnership between
Church and State, it is extremely
difficult justly to separate the interests of the Church and the State.
For instance, there are a number
of charitable and educational trusts
which, under the Spanish government, were generally administered
by clerical agents. Some of these
trusts were probably purely civil
trusts, others were probably religious trusts, and an issue of the
utmost nicety is presented when
decision must be given as to which
are civil and which are religious
trusts, so that the one may be administered under the Government
of the United States and the other

[119]

by the Roman Catholic Church.
Again, under the agreement between the Spanish Crown and the
Church, the government furnished
compensation for the priests, and
also agreed to aid in the construction of churches and so-called conventos or priests' rectories. So
close was the relation between the
Church and the State that it was
not thought necessary to obtain a
patent from the government to the
bishop of the diocese for the public
land upon which the church and
rectory were built, so that probably
a majority of the churches and rectories of the island (and there are
a church and a rectory in nearly
every pueblo in the island) stand

upon what the records show to be public land, and which, as such, passed to the Government of the United States under the Treaty of Paris. In such a case, however, it may very well be urged that while the legal title is in the Government, the equitable title is in the Catholics of the parish, and that, in accordance with the canonical law, releases should be made by the Government of the United States to the bishop of the diocese for the benefit of the Catholics of the parish. In some pueblos, however, the municipalities claim an interest in the conventos, and indeed in the churches, on the ground that they furnished the labor or material with which the churches and rectories were constructed, and in some instances they have attempted to assert an ownership in these buildings. Indeed, it is very hard for the common people to understand the principle of the separation of Church and State, and much time of the Civil Governor is taken up in explaining to the municipal authorities that they have no right as such to regulate the conduct of the priests in their churches or the fees which they charge. Again, the conventos or rectories have furnished the most convenient houses for occupation by the American soldiers during the guerrilla warfare, and in some instances, too, churches have been occupied as barracks. The question naturally arises whether rental is not due from the United States for such occupation of church property, and what the reasonable rental shall be. This question is complicated with another, and that is whether the fact that the priests may have aided and abetted the insurgents, and may have had many insurgents among their parishioners, may not disentitle the parishes to a recovery of reasonable rental. If a rental is due, it is important that it should be promptly paid, because the war has, of course, much reduced the source of income for the Church and impaired its usefulness in affording

[123]

opportunities for religious worship to the people.

The four orders of friars, the Dominicans, the Augustinians, the Recoletos, and the Franciscans, all of them Spaniards (for natives are not admitted to the orders), were the parish priests among the Christian Filipino people, and these orders, except the Franciscans, became the owners, through purchase and otherwise, of four hundred thousand acres of agricultural land, two hundred and fifty thousand of which are situated near the city of Manila, and include some of the richest land in the islands. The better lands lie in the populous provinces of Cavite, Laguna, Bulacan, old Manila (now Rizal), and Cebú. One hundred and twenty-five thousand acres lie in the province of Cavite, and it is significant that of the three revolutions against Spain (if that of 1870 can be called a revolution), all began in this province, showing that the agrarian question of the ownership of these lands by the friars, while it was not the only issue, had much to do with the dissatisfaction which led to the armed resistance to Spanish authority. Civil government has now been completely established in Bulacan, old Manila or Rizal, Cavite, and Cebú, and soon will be established in Laguna. The title of the friars to these lands is, from a legal standpoint, good. Indeed, there is probably no better title in the islands. Since 1896 no rents have been collected, and the former tenants have enjoyed the lands without price, so far as the conditions of war permitted. When now the friars shall call upon the ordinary courts of justice, as they have the right to do, either to collect the rents from their tenants or to restore them to the possession of their lands, the process of the court and the power of the government must be exerted to enforce the judgment which the proof of such facts will require. To an ignorant people, hostile to the friars, this will put the Government of the United States in the attitude of supporting the friars, and of siding with them in the controversy out of which grew the revolution against Spain, and there is every indication that riot and disturbance will follow any effort by the Government to aid the friars in the assertion of their property rights. It has been thought by the Commission to be the wisest policy, and one just to all interests, for the Government to purchase these lands from the friars, paying them a reasonable price therefor. Both the House and the Senate bills make provision for such purchase.

A somewhat perplexing compli-

cation has arisen by the transfer of
the title of the lands by the friars
to promoting companies or individuals for the purpose of their sale
or cultivation, but it is understood
that the friars have thus far re-
tained a controlling interest in each
corporation taking the lands, and
that they may, if they desire, sell
the lands to the Government.

Again, under the Spanish rule in
the Philippines the friars discharged
most important civil functions.
Great credit is due to the religious
orders for the work which they did
in Christianizing the Archipelago
and in bringing about the civilization which to-day exists in the isl-

[128]

ands, but in the last half-century the Spanish government, apparently without objection by the friars, imposed upon them extensive civil duties in connection with municipal and provincial governments, until substantially all the political power exercised in municipal governments became absorbed by the friars. The friar priest in each parish became the chief of police and the chief of detectives in government work. Every man who was punished, especially if he were punished for a political offense, charged it to the agency of the friar, and the deportations and executions which went on under Spanish rule were all laid at the door of the religious orders.

To the people of the pueblos the friar was the crown of Spain, and every oppression by the Spanish government was traced by them to the men whose political power had far outgrown that exercised by them as priests. When the revolution came, therefore, deep hostility was manifested by the insurgents against the friars. They had to flee for their lives. Fifty of them were killed and three hundred of them were imprisoned, and during their imprisonment were subjected to the most humiliating indignities and to the greatest suffering. The feeling of the people against the friars was wholly political. The people were generally good Catholics and enjoyed and wished for the sacraments of their Church. With a population such as that of the Christian Filipinos, with ninety per cent. so densely ignorant, speaking eight or ten different languages, it is hardly possible to say that there is any public opinion such as we understand it; but to this general remark must be made the exception that there is a universal popular hatred of the four religious orders which have been under discussion. It is entirely aside from the point to question the justice of this feeling. It exists and must be reckoned with by those who are charged with the responsibility of carrying on civil government in the islands. The friars were driven out of all the parishes in the Archipelago except those of the city of Manila, where the American forces have always been. A few of their number have returned to Cebú, to Vigan, and to Tuguegarao in the province of Cagayán, but the great body of them still remain in Manila and are unable to return to the parishes because of the expressed hatred of the people. If they should attempt to return in any numbers, it is quite likely that the result would be disturbance and riot.

Such religious worship as is now carried on in the parishes is conducted by native priests who were

in the Spanish times the assistants
or deputies of the friars. There
are not enough of these priests to
supply the needs of all the parishes, even if they were entirely
satisfactory to the Church; and the
necessity in the interest of the
Church of furnishing additional
priests is, I think, recognized in
the islands. The difficulty which
the Church has in finding competent priests that are available for
service in the islands must be admitted. Of course it would accord
with the views of the Americans if
American Catholic priests could be
sent to the islands, because their
high standard and their knowledge
of how a Church may thrive and

[133]

gain strength under a government in which Church and State are entirely separate would assist much in establishing the new order of things with the people. But it is said that there is no supply of American Catholic priests which can fill this demand.

The question which is presented to the civil government of the islands is whether there is not some means of avoiding the lawlessness and riot which the friars' return to their parishes is certain to involve. Of course the civil government has nothing to do with the ministrations of religion or with the personnel of the agents selected by the Church to conduct its worship, so long as

they are law-abiding and do not
preach treasonable doctrine ; but it
cannot but give the greatest concern to the civil government if a
Church shall adopt the policy of
sending among the people priests
whose very presence is sure to involve disturbance of law and order.
With a people so ignorant and having a knowledge only of Spanish
methods of government, the return
of the friars will necessarily be
regarded as due to an affirmative
policy on the part of the government, and the burden of hostility
which the friars now bear will necessarily be shared by the government.   If the purchase of the lands
of the friars and the adjustment of

all the other questions arising between the Church and the State should include a withdrawal of the friars from the islands, it would greatly facilitate the harmony between the government and the people and between the Church and the State.

I have stated some of the principal questions arising between the Church and the State for the purpose of showing the great advantage which will be attained should these differences be settled by amicable adjustment between the Church and the State. In such a matter, were we dealing with a secular corporation, it would seem a wiser policy and a more American and direct method of doing business to deal with the chief authority in the corporation rather than with some agent having but limited powers. The Administration has concluded that the advantage of the direct method and the possibility of settling the differences amicably with the Church by such a method warrant it in running the risk of the unjust criticism that such negotiation involves the establishment of diplomatic relations with the Vatican, and a departure from the traditions of our Government in this regard. Instead of being a departure from such traditions, such a negotiation seems to be an indis-

[137]

pensable condition precedent to the proper separation of the interests of Church and State in the Philippines. The unusual circumstance of a transfer of sovereignty from a government whose interests were almost indissolubly united to the Church, to a government whose interests must be kept separate from the Church, is what makes the proposed negotiation necessary. It is true that some of the questions might be settled by litigation, but a judicial settlement of them will involve long delay, consequent irritation, and possible charges of partiality against the courts which are finally called upon to decide the controversies. Is it not wiser, if it be possible, to settle all the questions by a friendly arrangement, and thus assist both the State and the Church in the pursuit of their proper aims for the benefit and uplifting of the Filipino people? It is possible that the views of the Administration and the views of the Church authorities may be so widely different as to the proper course to pursue that other methods of settlement must be found, but it is hoped that the great common interest which the Church and the State have in reaching a settlement will lead to such concessions on each side as will make it possible. The wise and enlightened statesmanship which has characterized the long and prosperous pontificate of Leo XIII. furnishes just ground for this hope.

A difficulty which may possibly confront the Philippine Government is the success of the Democratic party in the next Congressional elections. This will be taken in the Philippines as an indication that at the end of the present Administration the policy of the United States will be changed and the islands will be abandoned by the United States and turned over to a government to be established by the people of the islands through the calling of a constitutional convention. The prospect of such a

change will have a tendency to
paralyze the energy of the conservative element of the Filipino people
who are now assisting us in the
maintenance of a civil government
in the islands, and all will be sus-
pense and agitation. This difficulty, however, is inherent in the
government of dependent posses-
sions by a Republic like our own
whenever the chief political issue
between the parties is the policy to
be pursued with respect to such dependencies. I venture to think,
however, that should the Republi-
can party be successful in the Congressional elections next following
and in the next National election,
sufficient progress will be made in

the solution of the problem of the Philippine Government to insure the removal of the main issue from practical politics thereafter.